BREAKING
THE POWER OF
THE Past

behind YOU,
lies the
liabilities
of your
"ancestry"

Dr. D. K. Olukoya

Breaking The Power of The Past

© 2014 DR. D. K. OLUKOYA

ISBN:

Published December, 2014

Published by:
The Battle Cry Christian Ministries
322, Herbert Macaulay Street, Sabo, Yaba
P. O. Box 12272, Ikeja, Lagos.
www.battlecrystore.com
email: info@battlecrystore.com
        customercare@battlecrystore.com
        sales@battlecrystore.com
Phone: 0803-304-4239, 0816-122-9775

I salute my wonderful wife, Pastor Shade, for her invaluable support in the ministry.
I appreciate her unquantifiable support in the book ministry as the cover designer, art editor and art adviser.

All the Scriptures are from the King James Version

CONTENTS

Breaking The Power of the Past

The past has great influence on the present and the future. Your past can affect your destiny. Your past can imprison your future. Your past can render your future useless. Your past can rise up like Goliath and stand in the way of your future. Your past can subject you to terrible harassment. If care is not taken, the arrows you received in the past can render your tomorrow impotent. You must deal with your past if you want to succeed in life.

THE STRENGTH OF THE PAST

Until you realise the strength of the past, you may not be able to successfully secure the future. The past is so stubborn that it can trouble your present and your future persistently. No one can afford to underestimate the power of the past. The past may appear gone and forgotten but the grim consequences will continue to linger. No one may know what happened in the past, but, by looking at your present situation, it is possible to detect what probably took place in the past.

The stories of your ancestors might have been long forgotten, but what is happening in the present generation is a clear reflection of your ancestral past. Trees form an important aspect of vegetation in our environment. whether it is a Mahogany tree or an Iroko tree, the same features are retained for a very long time. The lesson from the foregoing is that every human being on earth belongs to an ancestry. You are part of a family tree that dates back to hundreds of years.

What is characteristic of family trees is that members of the family share something in common. The trees are made up of branches and each branch is very important. There is a root that holds the tree together. Without the root there will be no tree. As stated earlier, trees do not change their features. Hence, the evil deposits in your branch (life) brought in by your family tree will remain there unless something is done about it.

The battle with the past must be fought and won. Unless you paralyse the power of the past, it might paralyse you. You must come up against the power of the past spiritually. This is one of the toughest battles to fight. I want you to prepare yourself for the battle. Make use of these powerful confessions. It will set the battle in motion. You will become a winner. It will unleash the spirit of a champion upon you. Lay your hands on your chest and make this pronouncement.

YOUR PERSONAL CONFESSION

I am Daniel Olukoya (put your own names here). I stand here today and I decree by the decree of heaven that I shall arise by fire and shine. Any power pressing down my head I bury you alive, in the name of Jesus.

By the blood of Jesus and by the fire of God, I shall not carry over any evil thing, in the name of Jesus. Holy Ghost, come upon me. Power of the Most High, overshadow my life. Say amen seven times.

The miracle that will make you to be celebrated shall suddenly manifest, in the name of Jesus.
I decree that the breakthrough that will announce your celebration shall break forth through this book, in the name of Jesus. The celebration and thanksgiving that will announce the power of God in your life shall start today, in the name of Jesus. Your enemies shall be put to shame. Anywhere the enemy has closed any door against

you, the power of the God of Elijah shall open the door, in the name of Jesus. As you continue to read this book you must pay attention so that you can achieve a good grasp of this important topic.

STAGES OF LIFE
The life of a man is divided into three stages
1. Your yesterday.
2. Your today.
3. Your tomorrow.

For the sake of clarity you can also look at the life of man in these three dimensions.
1. Your past.
2. Your present.
3. Your future.

Yesterday is a total embodiment of your past. Today is a description of what is happening in your life at the moment. The future is a promissory note. There is no human being who has power over the past, present and future. There is no great man anywhere who can control the past, the present and the future. There is not much anyone can do about the past. The realities of today are difficult to handle. The future is so unpredictable that no one can have a firm grip of it. But beloved, I have good news for you. There is someone who can take absolute control of your past, your present and your future. The Bible declares; Jesus Christ is the same yesterday, today, and forever.

Jesus is the only one who knows your past, your present and your future. He remains the only one who can go into the three realms of your life and boldly declare "Son/daughter I am the same yesterday today and forever". Jesus speaks with authority. Your past can not frighten Him. Your present cannot make Him afraid. Your future cannot intimidate Him. He is the only one who can break the power of the past. He is the only one who has surveyed your past and your present and can tell you that your tomorrow will be alright. When Jesus is in charge of your life, all shall be well.

A SCRIPTURAL SURVEY

Let us examine the power of the past by reading some scriptures.

1 Samuel 2:30-36:

"Wherefore the LORD God of Israel saith, I said indeed that thy house, and the house of thy father,

should walk before me for ever: but now the LORD saith, Be it far from me; for them that honour me I will honour, and they that despise me shall be lightly esteemed. Behold, the days come, that I will cut off thine arm, and the arm of thy father's house, that there shall not be an old man in thine house. And thou shalt see an enemy in my habitation, in all the wealth which God shall give Israel: and there shall not be an old man in thine house for ever. And the man of thine, whom I shall not cut off from mine altar, shall be to consume thine eyes, and to grieve thine heart: and all the increase of thine house shall die in the flower of their age. And this shall be a sign unto thee, that shall come upon thy two sons, on Hophni and Phinehas; in one day they shall die both of them. And I will raise me up a faithful priest, that shall do according to that which is in mine heart and in my mind: and I will build him a sure house; and he shall walk before mine anointed for ever. And it shall come to pass, that every one that is left in thine house shall come and crouch to him for a piece of silver and a morsel of bread, and shall say, Put me, I pray thee, into one of the priests' offices, that I may eat a piece of bread."

Eli had caused a great deal of trouble. He had children and grandchildren. He caused trouble in his family tree. The curse placed on him went down to every member of his lineage. There was a power in the past of the children of Eli that was responsible for cutting people off in the prime of their age.

I pray for you that you shall receive deliverance now from the enemy that is plaguing your family with untimely death in the name that is above every other name, Jesus Christ, the Son of the Living God.

PRAYER SECTION

1. Blood of Jesus, invade my past and consume every demonic yoke in the name of Jesus

2. Ancestral limiting chains, break by fire in the name of Jesus

3. Any evil flow from my past, be cut off by the blood of Jesus, in the name of Jesus

4. Evil effects of my yesterday, on my destiny, dry up in the name of Jesus

5. Jesus, the same yesterday, today and forever, repackage my life by signs and wonders in the name of Jesus

The Mystery of Evil Inheritance

> *"The LORD is longsuffering, and of great mercy, forgiving iniquity and transgression, and by no means clearing the guilty, visiting the iniquity of the fathers upon the children unto the third and fourth generation."* **Numbers 14:18**

GENERATIONAL CURSES

Generational curses are real. Problems can pass through generations and trouble the offsprings. What your parents did can affect you and future generations. If your father or grandfather was either a thief, a drunkard, a womaniser, or someone who struggled with bad temper, whether he is alive or dead, you can be affected by it today.

In the same vein, if your mother happens to be a talkative, a sickler or someone who was lazy, you can also be affected whether she is dead or alive.

You should also take note of your paternal or maternal ancestors' weaknesses and negative traits. You are also likely to be affected by the deficits in their lives. You need details of the evil family trees if you must deal with them. When you take note of the common problems in their lives, you might be able to trace the problems you are going through today to them.

Isaiah 14:21 says;
"Prepare slaughter for his children for the iniquity of their fathers; that they do not rise, nor possess the land, nor fill the face of the world with cities."

This is a very powerful passage. Here, we are told that the children will not be able to rise because of their past. Today, many people are struggling with backwardness and demotion due to ancestral problems and pollution.

Job 21:19:
"God layeth up his iniquity for his children: he rewardeth him, and he shall know it."

Here, we are told that judgement can be reserved for the children because of the evil deeds of their ancestors. Evil rewards can be passed on to innocent children as a result of what their parents did, even when the children are not aware of them at all.

2 Samuel 12:9-11:

"Wherefore hast thou despised the commandment of the LORD, to do evil in his sight? thou hast killed Uriah the Hittite with the sword, and hast taken his wife to be thy wife, and hast slain him with the sword of the children of Ammon. Now therefore the sword shall never depart from thine house; because thou hast despised me, and hast taken the wife of Uriah the Hittite to be thy wife. Thus saith the LORD, Behold, I will raise up evil against thee out of thine own house, and I will take thy wives before thine eyes, and give them unto thy neighbour, and he shall lie with thy wives in the sight of this sun."

GREAT DEFICITS

This is a terrible curse. By virtue of what happened in the past, future generations are made to suffer. As long as the offsprings of David continue to increase and multiply, cases of murder will be rampant. This curse was so devastating that it was meant to affect even unborn children. Do you know that David was forgiven? But, the consequences remained. He was cursed but forgiven.

Matthew 27:24-25:

"When Pilate saw that he could prevail nothing, but that rather a tumult was made, he took water, and washed his hands before the multitude, saying, I am innocent of the blood of this just person: see ye to it."

Here, we see parents who made a pronouncement that affected innocent children. The children were not there when the fathers made a self-inflicted curse. The forefathers issued the curse and several years later, the children were affected. Many people today are facing hard battles. It is simply because many of these people are yet to pacify their angry past. The past of many people is roaring in violent anger. You have not pacified your past. You are yet to deal with it. That is why you are facing tough or hard battles.

EVIL INHERITANCE

Recently, a man who happened to be the only surviving child approached me for spiritual help and prayers. He narrated how his father called him and told him that out of all the 25 children that he had, he was the one he liked most. He went ahead to warn him that he must not accept any part of his inheritance when he dies. His father told him, "I am sure that you know that I am stinkingly rich. But I must inform you that all my wealth was obtained from the kingdom of darkness.

Whoever took part of it would be writing letters to trouble, curses and calamities. The father warned the man. By the time the father died, there was a lot of money to share. There were lots of houses to share. But since the young man had been warned, he rejected everything he was offered.

While the property was being shared, everyone thought the young man was crazy. All the other 24 children of his late father got fantastic shares. But right now, all the 24 children are now dead. The only survivor is the young man who refused to touch his father's money and properties.

My prayer for you is that any covenant that your ancestors made with the kingdom of darkness that wants to terminate your destiny shall be terminated and the Lord shall deliver you, in the name of Jesus.

I ministered to someone else recently. In her own case her father happened to be a witch doctor. The father had 12 children and refused to send anyone of them to school. With 12 children who could neither read nor write living with him, whenever a letter was sent to him, he often sought the assistance of the children of his neighbours to help him read the letters. Anyone of his children who tried to make personal efforts to educate himself or herself died in the process.

One of them tried to be educated by enrolling for an adult education class. Unfortunately, the first day he started the lesson, he had a ghastly accident and died instantly. By the spirit of God, I declare that every negative covenant made by your forefathers against your destiny is hereby cancelled, in the name of Jesus.

I want you to be aware of the fact that, the past of many people grows furious by the day. It is tragic when people struggle with a past that is violently angry. When your past is furious and seeking means of vengeance, it is dangerous. It is not possible to ignore the past. It is highly impossible to spiritually sweep the past under the carpet. The past is a stubborn reality. The voice of the past is extremely stubborn. Unless there is divine intervention, the scars of the past are indelible. Once negative things are in place they will continue to bring up unpleasant consequences, whether the victim is aware or not.

PRAYER SECTION

1.   I disconnect my life from every evil inheritance in the name of Jesus

2.   Ancestral mistakes and iniquities affecting my life now, be silenced by the blood of Jesus

3.   Hidden curses, from my past be nullified by the blood of Jesus

4.   Mercy of God, deliver my ancestral line in the name of Jesus

5.   I come out of the darkness of my father's house by fire in the name of Jesus

The Crying Past

Beloved, you cannot afford to turn blind eyes on your past. Everything, whether a person, a place or a thing, has a past. If you are ignorant of the past you continue to be ignorant of the future. If you know nothing about the past, the future may look confusing. No matter how hard we try, it is impossible to erase the past.

To correctly define the future, research into the past. Even if you decide to forget your past, your past will remember you; especially if you have formed any pact or any covenant with the enemy secretly or openly. The past is a vagabond. It never stays where you left it. You cannot know where you are going, if you never know where you have been.

If you fail to deal with the power of the past, it will deal with you. There is definitely no future without the past. Beloved, no man is free from his history. The negative past lies upon man like a giant dead body. The past is a terror.

When you allow the deficit of the past to remain, the profit you make in the future will be spent servicing the debts of the past.

The past is a researcher. The past is a lecturer. There is no freedom from the past. Beloved, the error of the past is the wisdom for your future. When you are completely ignorant of the past, you will be sentenced to repeat the same class over and over. The present is an egg laid by Mrs Past. Sooner or later, the egg will hatch offsprings that will trouble your future. To be an architect of your future, you must be released from the power of the past.

THE STUBBORN LEG

Many are struggling to move forward. But, unfortunately the past has placed one leg on the brake of the vehicle of their destiny. I pray for you right now that, whatever your ancestors have done that is placing a stubborn leg on the brake of your destiny, shall be wiped off by the blood of Jesus, today. In the spirit realm, nothing goes off automatically.

No amount of wishful thinking can erase the past. The past cannot be eradicated by imagination, neither can it disappear by speculation. The only way you can deal with your dark past is to use the weapon of war and fire. You must deal with your past right now.

The past can ruin a new beginning. It can rubbish your present efforts and convert you to someone who does not know what he or she is doing. Raise your right hand and make this prophetic declaration.

Every evil past break away from my future, in the name of Jesus.

I prophesy upon your life, from today your past will no longer prevent you from going forward, in the name of Jesus. God will give you a future that is better than your past. You will have a happy fresh start, in the name of Jesus.

You will receive deliverance from the stigma of the past, in the name of Jesus. The devil might have had the past, but I decree that he will never have your future, in Jesus' name. All the demons from the past, that have been holding you and preventing you from obtaining God's best, I bind them and cast them out, in the name of Jesus.

THE IMPORTANCE OF THE PAST

In the past of many, there are angry pursuing masquerades. Several pasts are filled with agents that pursue. Many have struggled with the past with the rage of the wicked. Others have been pursued by wicked avengers. There are people whose pasts are occurrences of the crying blood. It is also possible that your wicked household has been crying against you from the past. It is possible that evil curses from the past are crying against you.

It is also possible that evil covenants from the past are crying against you today. What you are going through might be the cry of marital attacks from your past. If you take a look at your family tree and discover that no one ever had a settled marriage, you might also be a victim of the cry of wicked masquerades in your family line.

Again, you might be a victim of household enemies from your background. You might also be a victim of common besetting sins crying against you from your lineage. You could be going through the evil cry of inherited bondage from your past. You could also be suffering as a result of inherited bondage.

You could be suffering from the Jonah syndrome. God could have called your father or grandfather into the ministry, instead of obedience there was refusal. Perhaps, God also called you and you have also refused.

God is now dealing with you the way He dealt with your father. What you are going through might be due to the attacks of the power of the wasters from the past. Again, what you are suffering from could be coming from the powers of the emptier from the past.

Again, it is quite possible that anti-prosperity powers from your past are dealing with you. Your present travails might be as a result of evil strongholds that have dealt with your lineage from generation to generation.

THE RAGE OF THE PAST

A strong man from the past might be on a revenge mission against you. What you are going through could be attributed to the problem of closed doors that characterised the lives of your ancestors. Again, it could be the problem of recurrent battles at the edge of breakthroughs in your ancestry. You could be going through embargoes by witchcraft powers; problems that were prevalent among the forefathers. Who knows, you may also be experiencing the problems of environmental attacks which your fore fathers also experienced. You could be suffering also as a result of the attack of star hunters against you in the past.

Additionally, the rage of children killers arising from the innocent children killed by your forefathers in the past could be invoked against you by wicked ancestral powers. The power of infirmity that gave your ancestors sleepless nights could have decided to face you and molest your health. It is possible that you are facing the attacks of dream criminals from the past. It is also possible to come under the attacks of the spirit of seduction from the past.

What you are going through can also be attributed to attacks from powers that make people fall from grace to grass. Your present situation could have been engineered by angry masquerades your forefathers worshipped that you have refused to worship; who felt abandoned. Any masquerade of the past pursuing you and making you restless shall be buried today, in the name of Jesus.

Dealing with the power of the past will grant you uncommon deliverance. When you invoke the release of God's astonishing powers to deal with the power of the past, your destiny will begin to shine.

PRAYER SECTION

1. Every blood crying against me from my past, be silenced by the blood of Jesus

2. Known and unknown covenants, binding me to any evil history break by fire in the name of Jesus

3. Accusations from my past, delaying my congratulations today, shut up and die in the name of Jesus

4. Mighty hands of God break the evil yokes of my past life in the name of Jesus

5. Holy Ghost arise, connect me to my glory in the name of Jesus

Deep Questions

4

Everyone on earth belongs to a family. A community or a nation is made up of family units. The family can be likened to a tree with roots and branches. Immediately, there is any form of pollution arising from sinful acts engaged in by one's forefathers, the family tree will no longer be wholesome.

One negative deed done by a single member of one's ancestral lineage can put the family tree into generational problems. One bad spot in the family tree is enough to affect the family tree negatively. Until you utter an aggressive cry against family tree pollution, your destiny may remain traumatised.

As you cry against the pollution in your family tree, the Lord will give you uncommon breakthroughs, in the name of Jesus.

Deuteronomy 29:18:

"Lest there should be among you man, or woman, or family, or tribe, whose heart turneth away this day from the LORD our God, to go and serve the gods of these nations; lest there should be among you a root that beareth gall and wormwood;"

GALL AND WORMWOOD

A man can be a root that bears gall and wormwood. In the same vein, a woman may be the root that injects gall and wormwood. It is also possible for a tribe to be likened to a root that bears gall and wormwood. When there is gall and wormwood in the root, it will surely spread into the lives of every member who forms part of the family tree. Herein lies the answer to the deep questions that many people are asking today.

Questions are crucial to the discovery of deep things in life. The only person that the devil fears is someone who is asking the right questions. As long as you are busy asking the wrong questions, the devil will ignore you; as the answers which you are going to get will not affect him in anyway. If a snake bites someone and the person is busy asking to know where the snake came from rather than quickly deal with the poison of the snake already in the body, the person is asking the wrong question. Where the snake came from does not matter. What matters is the step you must take to deal with the poison of the snake already in the body.

As long as the enemy has successfully diverted your attention and made you to get busy asking the wrong question, you cannot win destiny's battle. The enemy will not be bothered about the answers you are going to get. The questions you ask determine your destiny.

The kind of research you undertake following the questions you asked will determine your success or failure in life. If you are pursuing the wrong destiny ignorantly, the devil will not feel threatened at all. If you close your eyes to your past and ignore the consequences of ignorance, the enemy will succeed at dribbling you. When you live as if there is no past or when you go about the journey of life as if whatever happens in the past can never affect your present and your future, the devil will continue to determine your destiny like one playing a juvenile ball.

THE MOUNTAIN OF IGNORANCE

Every man's mountain is that of his ignorance. If you want to attain and achieve your divine destiny, you must begin with serious personal questions. The questions you ask determine the type of destiny you are going to have. Good questions determine good destiny. Your seeds of success are tucked away in the kind of answers you get when you ask good questions. You must bombard your life with result oriented questions. You must face yourself squarely and ask questions like:

1. Who am I?
2. Where do I come from?
3. Where is my destination?
4. How much ground have I covered as far as the journey of life is concerned?
5. Am I pursuing my destiny?
6. What will I gain from the steps I have taken so far?

To get answers that will open the doors of destiny, you need to come up with appropriate questions. Someone said "He who asks questions can only be a fool for five minutes. But, he who does not ask remains a fool forever." It is better to keep asking several questions than to keep mute and miss your way. It is better to be accused of asking too many questions than miss the way and get lost because you refused to ask questions.

WHEN YOU ASK QUESTIONS

Recently time a young man won a scholarship and had to travel abroad came to me and asked; "Dr. Daniel Olukoya, do you have any advice for me?" I asked to know if he ever travelled before. He humbly told me that it was his first time of travelling out of the country. Then I opened up and told him; "Since where you are going is so far away, I have one piece of advice for you; ask questions. Whatever you are doing and wherever you are, keep asking questions. The more you ask questions the more you will be guided. He thanked me, made preparations and went to the international airport on the date of departure.

While he was at the airport he was busy asking questions. Hence, he got everything right. By the time he left Nigeria and there was a transit connection in another country, he stopped asking questions. He made the greatest mistake of his life by believing that he did not need to let anyone know that he was ignorant of travel arrangements during a connecting flight. He decided to put two and two together to make four. He just joined the nearest queue.

Unfortunately, the queue he settled for was not going towards his destination. Before he could realise what was happening, the aircraft he was supposed to board had left. But if he had continued asking questions, he would not have been stranded.

A LOOK AT TWO FAMILIES IN HISTORY

Wise questions can conquer so many troubles. Asking questions constitute the ABC of diagnosis. It is only a man who stops asking questions that becomes a fool. If there is any root that bears gall and wormwood and you are completely ignorant, things will continue to go wrong. Someone carried out a research several years ago and came out with shocking findings. He studied a particular family tree and thoroughly observed each member of the family. The research bordered on a man called Mac Jukes.

Mac Jukes was an ungodly man. He was an atheist who got married to an ungodly woman. The researcher thoroughly examined the life of 550 descendants of Mac Jukes. He discovered that in the family tree of Mac Jukes 310 died as paupers. 150 became hardened criminals. Seven of the descendants ended up as murderers, 100 members of Mac Jukes' family were certified chronic drunkards. More than half of the women from that family were prostitutes. The research findings made it clear that Mac Jukes family was a deficit to the government of the United States of America.

There was another man who lived during the time of Mac Jukes. Interestingly, the man was a sharp contrast to Mac Jukes. The same researcher picked on the family of Jonathan Edwards. Jonathan

Edwards was a man of God who, with his household served the living God. Jonathan Edwards happened to be one of the greatest preachers who ever lived. He was the famous preacher of the sermon titled; "Sinners in the hands of an angry God." That sermon remains the most powerful message that God ever used mortal man to preach.

The message was so powerful that listeners had to grab the poles of the auditorium, lest the ground on which they stood caved in and they sank into hell.

Jonathan Edwards served God in His own generation. He raised a godly family. His grandchildren also served God faithfully. He was probably the first man in Christian history to take an altar call. He had a total of 1,094 descendants. The researchers made the following findings. Out of his family and descendants:

1. 295 became college presidents.
2. 65 were university professors.
3. Three of his children were elected as senators in the United States of America.
4. 3 were state Governors.
5. 30 were judges.
6. 100 were lawyers.

7. One of them became the Dean of a great faculty.
8. 75 became great military officers who served meritoriously in the army of the United States of America.
9. 100 were well known missionaries, preachers and authors.
10. One of his children was the officer in charge of the treasury of the United States of America.

None of the descendants of Jonathan Edwards was a liability to the United States of America. This shows that your family tree will either give you generational blessings or it can give you generational problems.

I pray for you that any termite that is hiding in your family tree shall be destroyed by fire, in the name of Jesus.

PRAYER SECTION

1:    Holy Ghost arise and reveal deep secrets about my past to me in the name of Jesus

2.   Every hold of darkness on my family line, break off in the name of Jesus

3.   I announce the obituary of the ghost from my past in the name of Jesus

4.   I refuse to live in ignorance about my past in the name of Jesus

5.   Every veil of darkness hiding beneficial information from me, catch fire in the name of Jesus

Your Family Life and Your Destiny

Matthew 27:24-30:

"When Pilate saw that he could prevail nothing, but that rather a tumult was made, he took water, and washed his hands before the multitude, saying, I am innocent of the blood of this just person: see ye to it. Then answered all the people, and said, His blood be on us, and on our children. Then released he Barabbas unto them: and when he had scourged Jesus, he delivered him to be crucified. Then the soldiers of the governor took Jesus into the common hall, and gathered unto him the whole band of soldiers. And they stripped him, and put on him a scarlet robe. And

when they had platted a crown of thorns, they put it upon his head, and a reed in his right hand: and they bowed the knee before him, and mocked him, saying, Hail, King of the Jews! And they spit upon him, and took the reed, and smote him on the head."

It is possible that someone in your family line had issued curses under which you now labour. If you have been labouring under malignant family curses, they are hereby revoked and your offsprings are excluded, in Jesus' name. Unfortunately, consequences of curses are suffered by succeeding generations. The people who crucified Jesus made a pronouncement: "His blood be on us, and on our children." The punishment for the pronouncement came to pass in AD 70 when General Titus invaded Jerusalem and destroyed the entire city. In that invasion, General Titus killed seven million Jews. According to the records of respected Jewish historians, enemy soldiers ripped open the stomach of pregnant women, removed unborn babies and dashed their heads on the wall. During the invasion, one rich Jew decided to get smart by swallowing all his gold coins and started running thinking that he would escape with his wealth. One of the soldiers of General Titus threw a javelin at him and it hits his stomach, His stomach was ripped open and gold coins began to fall off from his stomach. From that moment, whenever the soldier saw any Jew with protruding stomach, javelins were aimed at their stomachs, and many lives were lost.

YOUR PAST AND YOUR FUTURE

The ancestors of the Jews pronounced a curse upon them. They suffered the consequences of their pronouncement. That was not the end of the ordeals of the children of Israel. Many years later, a man called Adolf Hitler unleashed his anger against the Jews. Someone had said that Adolf Hitler's father was a bastard son of a Jewish landlord who made a lady pregnant. Hitler's father was badly treated by the Jewish landlord. Hence, Hitler grew up with serious hatred against Jews. It is on record that Hitler killed about six million Jews. Innocent Jews suffered in the hands of Hitler. The children of Israel suffered a lot of atrocities from the hands of Hitler because of what their ancestors did.

There was a young man, several years ago, who was physically handicapped. He approached his father for help but the father refused to help him. The boy was eventually sent to a psychiatric home where he was taken care of. There, the young man met a beautiful lady and got married to her. The girl became pregnant.

Unfortunately, tragedy struck at the time of delivery. The young man's wife died during childbirth. The young man was so devastated by the tragedy of losing his wife. When the young man examined his physical disability and the loss of his wife, he committed suicide. Although, the baby survived. There were two serious disabilities. The baby suffered from physical and mental disabilities.

In spite of the disabilities, the baby grew up and became an adult. One day, mentally retarded people and people with other disabilities were brought together and a group was formed to welcome the president of the United States of America. As the American President was about shaking the disabled baby that had become a man, suddenly, something went wrong and the disabled man brought out a gun and shot the American President. The crippled boy was sentenced to die by hanging. He was executed, that was how an entire family was wiped off. This is a serious matter.

PRAYING AGAINST A SIEGE

In 1994, a brother rushed to us because the spirit of death had almost finished all the members of his family. Within six months, they had lost 19 members of the family. Only two of them remained alive. We told them that eaters of flesh and drinkers of blood were on the rampage.

I specifically told them not to travel at all. I gave them prayer points to pray in order to arrest the tide of death. When I was talking to both of them, the younger brother was barely listening to me. When they were supposed to start the prayer programme I apportioned to them, the younger brother insisted that he was going to go back to the village to pick up money and materials he kept in their country home.

The elder brother warned the younger one against travelling or going home but the young man insisted that nothing would make him change his mind. The elder brother was left alone to pray.

The elder brother started the prayer session exactly 9pm and continued till 12 midnight. Immediately, it was few minutes past midnight, the Lord gave him a startling revelation.

All of a sudden, an army of fearful soldiers rushed towards him throwing all kinds of things against him. He told me that the only time he heard such frightening gunshots was at the time of the Nigerian civil war. He noticed that as they were firing at him, a man in dazzling white robes appeared between him and the soldiers parrying the bullets away.

The bombardment was so terrible that the younger brother who stubbornly travelled to the village met with tragedy while he was coming back. A petrol tanker collided with the vehicle he was travelling in. The result was instant death.

The accident was so terrible that even his ashes could not be gathered for burial. The elder brother survived because he was obedient. The younger brother became a victim of the eaters of flesh and the drinkers of blood who were in that family.

GENERATIONAL CURSES

Beloved, if every crime that makes headlines in our newspapers were investigated, you would discover that those who carried out such crimes have serious problems with their family trees. I read an interesting story concerning a woman of African origin called Anita Ngako. She went through serious ordeals. She revealed that for four years, a strange horn kept growing at the centre of her head giving her agonising headaches.

She became curious and started serious investigations about her ancestry. To her surprise, she discovered that her great, great grand-father was an African witch doctor who also had, according to family history, a horn in his head. Four generations later, the horn had come back to hunt Anita Ngako.

Strange things are happening in this world. A lot of abnormalities are happening in the lives of children which parents cannot explain. Most of the time, it is because someone in the family line had sown a bad seed.

PRAYER SECTION

1: Unprofitable agreement made by my parents on my behalf, be revoked in the name of Jesus

2. By fire, by fire, I release myself from evil dedications, in the name of Jesus

3. Collective captivity of my family line, be destroyed by fire in the name of Jesus

4. Unused glory of my father's house, lost opportunities of my father's house, manifest in my life in the name of Jesus

5. Whatever is pulling my life backward, break and catch fire in the Jesus' name

6

Your Root and Your Destiny

At this point, I want you to spend a few minutes to pray. Here is the prayer point:

Powers in my roots, troubling my destiny, die, in the name of Jesus. To research into your family lineage, you can ask the questions indicated below:

WHAT TYPE OF SINS ARE PECULIAR WITH YOUR FAMILY LINEAGE?

Every family lineage has peculiar besetting sins. You must understand your family's besetting sins. Each ancestral lineage's besetting sins attract some peculiar ancestral foundational problems. When some peculiar sins run in the blood of most members of the lineage, such sins will subject future generations to serious bondage. If you have discovered that the sins that are peculiar to your family often rear up their ugly heads, you need to pray and deal with such sins. Such sins are actually beyond you. They have been programmed into the genes of every member of the lineage. To be free, you must deal with your roots. In some families it is chronic lies, in some other families it is furious anger, in some other families it could be immorality. There are families where members struggle with compulsive stealing. If you belong to a family where some sins are peculiar or prominent, you need to pray hard and undergo deliverance. As long as the peculiar sins of your lineage are repeated in your own life, you will also partake in the bondage of your ancestors.

WHAT TYPE OF PECULIAR DISEASES ARE FOUND IN YOUR FAMILY LINEAGE?

There are strange occurrences in some families. Members just discover that some diseases go from one generation to another. There are families with regular occurrences of epilepsy. In some other families, it is insanity. In some families members grapple with coughs that defy medical treatment, in some families it could be stroke or paralyses at a certain age. What is peculiar about such diseases or ailments is that no matter the amount of medical treatment that is applied the diseases will remain intractable. The only solution is strong prayers and deliverance. You need to tackle such ancestral attacks in the area of health. To be free you must know your background. If you have struggled with strange health problems, it is an indication of the fact that you are a carrier of ancestral diseases or germs.

WHAT KIND OF TRAGEDY IS COMMON IN YOUR OWN FAMILY?

There are families in which there is a rise in the incidence of tragedies. When tragedies keep occurring in the lives of several family members, it is because there are problems in the roots of your family. The devil has programmed the occurrence of tragedies in many family lines. When such an evil programme is in place, there will be instances of tragedies, air disasters, auto crash, plane crash and sudden death of prominent family members.

Unfortunately, many people are suffering in this area. But, they have not been able to trace such tragedies to their ancestral roots. You must pray that God should open your eyes to discover tragedies in your ancestry. The moment the agenda of tragedy is spiritually dealt with in your lineage, such shall no longer occur in your personal life.

WHAT KIND OF IDOLS WERE OR ARE STILL BEING WORSHIPPED IN YOUR FAMILY?

The type of idols that were worshipped by your forefathers must be examined. Idols are spiritual entities. They demand various types of things. Some idols demand human blood, while others trigger calamities. Some are in charge of failure at the edge of breakthroughs. The idols which our forefathers worshipped, many years ago, are now busy asking for tithes to be paid to them. In some families, idols are still being worshipped. In some families the wicked idols that are worshipped often come up with strange demands. Unless such demands are met, all kinds of calamities will be triggered off. Since your forefathers worshipped idols, you are likely to reap the ugly fruits of idolatry.

IS YOUR FAMILY DEDICATED TO IDOLS?

A lot of families were dedicated to idols about 100 years ago. This dedication is still speaking negatively against them. Family dedication has put lots of Africans into bondage. When a particular family has been dedicated to a very powerful idol, all the members of the family will come under the influence of the idol. Family dedication places whole families under the umbrella of wicked idols. In the name of seeking for help, protection power or riches, our forefathers dedicated their lineage to the idols which they worshipped many years ago.

The consequences of dedications to idols are far reaching. As long as dedication is reflected, the idol remains glued to the members of the family. A lot of people often discover that they are under the rulership as well as the evil influence of the idols. You must personally cancel any dedication to idols that is working against you. You must dedicate yourself to Christ by saying no to being dedicated to idols by extension.

HAVE YOU DISCOVERED THAT NAMES THAT ARE DEDICATED TO IDOLS CAN BE FOUND IN YOUR EXTENDED FAMILY?

When family names are dedicated to idols, offsprings who bear such names will become carriers of evil burden and bondage. If the name of your family is any way affixed to the names of an idol, negative energy will flow from that idol to you since the idol has something to do with your surname. Idols are very jealous. They lay claim to the lives of those who share the same name with them. Even if it is in part or in full, the occurrence of names that are dedicated to idols in your family line is a reflection that your ancestors were chronic idol worshippers. Such names will keep on affecting all family members whether they are at home or abroad.

When idol worship is fully entrenched in the genealogy of a family line to the extent that names of powerful idols are the names that your ancestors bore, you must expect the demons to fight back or make certain demands at random. A lot of people display acute ignorance in this area. You cannot expect such idols to lie low and do nothing when your parents were named after them. Your family idols will do anything in order to show that their names cannot just be used in vain. Names are significant in the Bible. If your family name is attached to God, the Almighty will stand by your family members and do anything to defend His interest. You a true child of God, cannot afford to bear the names of the god of thunder, the ifa oracle and names of other wicked powerful idols.

WHAT KIND OF CURSES ARE PECULIAR TO YOUR FAMILY?

In the third world, especially in countries where there was serious idol worship, people entered evil covenants and consequently attracted curses. Members of many families will come under a siege as a result of the powerful curses that were pronounced against ancestors. There are various types of curses. Some curses are deadly while some other curses are so mobile that they follow family members, even when they travel abroad. In certain cases, curses are pronounced in order to keep members of a particular family under perpetual servitude.

WHICH OF THESE THINGS RUN IN YOUR FAMILY; DIVORCE, ENVY, ANGER, PRIDE, GREED, REJECTION OR SUICIDE?

It is possible for some negative current to keep running through your family. When such a thing happens, you will discover that things like divorce, inability to get married and marital instability are very common. You will notice that almost every member of the extended family is going through marital distress. In other families, anger, greed and pride would be noticed everywhere. In some other families there could be things like suicide tendencies. It will not just happen in the lives of a few family members, the trend could be found in the lives of most family members. Ladies from that family may keep jumping from one husband to another.

In some cases it is exactly what happened in the lives of parents that is happening in the lives of the children. It is as a result of the nature of the root of that particular lineage. Beloved, do not wait until the evil experiment is performed with your life.

You must quickly cancel the evil trait. You must not become part of the umbrella bondage of your family line. You must, as quickly as possible, deal with the negative trends in your family. Do not take them for granted. There are extended families where over ten people are said to have committed suicide after some time. If such problems are not dealt with, more suicide bids are bound to follow.

HAVE YOU DISCOVERED THAT WOMEN IN YOUR FAMILY OFTEN SUFFER GYNAECOLOGICAL PROBLEMS?

For some families the recurrent problem is gynaecological problems. Women keep experiencing problems in the area of conception. Those who manage to scale through the hurdle of conception end up battling with heart rendering miscarriages. Some members of such families experience still- births. Some family members generally face their own problems at the time of delivery. Mysterious things happen and babies are born with unexplainable deformities or abnormalities. Most of the time the gynaecological problems will gulp huge sums of money. Even when money is spent, results or solutions are difficult to come by. You need to undertake serious research.

IS UNTIMELY DEATH RAMPANT IN YOUR FAMILY?

There are families that are ravaged by untimely death. Most family members die prematurely. By the time men or women are close to age forty, they just die like chicken. The moment dark powers have sowed the seed of untimely death, death will become rampant. If you have examined your family and discovered that the major occurrence in your lineage is untimely death, you need to pray. To be quite honest with you, you need to go through deliverance.

IS POVERTY A COMMON ISSUE IN YOUR FAMILY?

There are families that are under the spell of poverty. By the time you take a look at the entire lineage, you will discover that almost everyone is struggling with poverty. In such a situation, the curse of poverty is in place. Those who manage to get rich and attain a level of comfort are mysteriously brought down to the level of poverty. If you have been praying for breakthroughs and prosperity and nothing is happening, you need to undertake serious research into your background and deal with the umbrella of poverty that has been placed over everyone in your ancestry. You must come out from the slave camp of poverty.

WHAT IS THE MEANING OF YOUR NAME?

To deal with your past, you need to examine your surname and your name. Often times, your personal name could be the door that has given the enemy a leeway to your life. If your name runs in sharp contrast to your prayers and profession, the devil may take advantage of you. If your name has been attracting bondage to your life, why not go for deliverance? If such a name has hindered you from moving into your glorious destiny, why not change such a name?

Names that are attached to the idols of your ancestors and names that bother on limitation or even curses must be discarded. God will give you a new name that will speak of His glory and attract His blessings. The meaning of your name must be looked into, if you want to cancel the negative influence of your past.

IS YOUR NAME ATTACHED TO IDOLS OR DEMONS?

One major way in which your destiny can be affected negatively is through associations with idols or demons. In those days, some names were given in order to exalt powerful idols. Some names are also given to reflect sources where children were obtained from after years of facing challenges in the area of childlessness. For example in some communities in Africa, couples go as far as making attempts to obtain children from the marine kingdom, the kingdom of cults and powerful local idols. Consequently, pledges are made and children are named in honour of the idols or the entities that rule the satanic kingdoms. Those who are given such names need serious deliverance.

HAVE YOU DISCOVERED SOME SIMILARITIES BETWEEN THE MEANING OF YOUR NAME AND YOUR ATITUDE?

Besides the problem faced by those who are named after idols, there are people who are given meaningless and sometimes negative names. Some names are so empty that it is difficult to decipher the real meaning. Sometimes some names are given as if the parents are cursing their children. Attitude like anger, stubbornness, sexual looseness, bad luck, vagrancy and other forms of unpleasant behaviour are subtly programmed into people's lives through their names. Consequently, some people discover that there is serious similarity between the meaning of their names and their attitude. You need to pray against the influence of names that are nearly useless.

DID YOU EVER PRACTICE OCCULTISM?

One of the problems of the past that is affecting many lives is involvement in the occult. If you ever dabbled into occultism and you are now born again, you are likely to experience lots of negative carry-overs. Even when you are no longer a devotee of occultism, you need to clear the cobwebs around your head due to past occult involvement. Yes, old things have passed away and all things have become new.

We must not overlook the fact that demonic powers will not easily let go. They will continue to hold on to past covenants and every old affinity. You must deal definitely and decisively with the effects of food consumed on the altar of the devil. Even when you have forgotten the past, occult powers are stubborn, they will not forget. You must renounce the power of the occult, cancel old covenants and dedicate your life to the Lord Jesus.

ARE THERE INSTANCES OF BLOODSHED IN YOUR FAMILY?

In most under developed and developing nations, there are instances of bloodshed in the ancestral past of almost everyone. There is no denying the fact that blood was shed during inter tribal wars and at the instances of communal clashes. Lots of rituals were carried out and most of them included bloodshed. Our forefathers pounded day old babies in the mortar in order to acquire fame, power and wealth. No doubt, our ancestors sure made use of human blood in their attempt to elongate their lives. In those days, to shed human blood was not a big deal. Some local and tribal heroes shed the blood of several children and adults in order to carry out rituals that would turn them to instant celebrities.

Years after the blood had been shed, succeeding generations may not know that the blood that their ancestors shed is speaking against them. If your ancestors were noted for shedding blood, you are bound to experience mysterious problems. Even if it has taken 100 years, the shed blood will never keep quiet. You can see why we emphasise what I term 'deep deliverance'. Cases that involved the shedding of blood require serious deliverance and prayers that border on the mercy of God.

HOW WAS THE FOUNDATION OF YOUR FAMILY HOUSE LAID?

One thing you must address is the issue of the foundation of your family. Of course, you might not be there when the foundation of your family house was laid. You might also know nothing concerning the charms, amulets and human parts that could have been buried when the foundation of your family house was laid. If you have spent decades in that family house, you need to go through deliverance. Such a foundation can affect your future or your destiny.

DO YOU KNOW WHAT WAS BURIED IN THE GROUND BEFORE THE FOUNDATION OF YOUR FAMILY HOUSE WAS LAID?

One of the areas to be considered when examining your roots or foundation is to examine what was probably buried in the ground before the foundation of your family house was laid. In those days, houses were not built ordinarily. The ground was often dug and all kinds of weird things were buried in the ground.

Although the purpose was achieved by our ancestors but they also attracted terrible problems and bondages for their offsprings. Every family member who lived in that building would pay costly prices sooner or later. If you happen to come from that kind of foundation or you were raised in that kind of building, you will need to go through deliverance.

ARE THERE CASES OF PREMATURE DEATHS IN YOUR FAMILY?

You also need to check out certain things in the area of premature death. Most people who died prematurely are under some evil spells as a result of the family they belonged to. When there is a pattern of premature death, members of such a family must quickly obtain spiritual help either through fervent prayers or outright deliverance. It is possible that several years ago, some incident, took place and some form of punishments were pronounced.

Consequently, there would be series of premature deaths. People would find it difficult to leave long unless such a precarious problem is addressed from spiritual standpoints. The situation will remain so even for generations yet to be born.

DO PEOPLE LIVE LONG OR DIE YOUNG?

One research you must undertake thoroughly is to find out whether people live long or die young. If people live long, it is a good trend in the family. However, when people always die at a young age, it is because they are under a deadly spiritual plague. It is a tragedy if the members of such a family leave things to blind chance. When members of the family die at infancy or at their youthful age there is a problem somewhere. The ugly trend must be addressed.

IS SUCCESS EASY TO ACHIEVE IN YOUR FAMILY?

One thing you must find out is whether success is easy to achieve or not. There are families where people sweat but they find it hard to achieve success. In some families, it is the problem of failure at the edge of success or breakthroughs. Somewhere along the line, some powers must have placed an embargo on the success of everyone from that family line.

DO MEMBERS OF YOUR FAMILY HAVE STABLE MARRIAGES?

When marriages are unstable there are spiritual undertones. Even when partners put in a lot of effort and there are no justifiable reasons why marriages should break up, members of some families keep on suffering terrible marital turbulence. When marital instability runs through an entire ancestry, it is a problem of evil roots. Even if members of that family are applying serious measures, the situation will remain intractable because spiritual forces are behind what has been happening. The solution is to tackle the problem from the root. This kind of umbrella bondage must be tackled once and for all.

IS THERE ANY CONSTANT PATTERN OF LATE MARRIAGE IN YOUR FAMILY?

This is a common problem in many families. Some families are bedevilled by the problem of lateness in marriage. Mysteriously, people find it hard to get married early. In most cases, people are still single when they are almost too old to find a suitor. Lateness in marriage is mostly caused by spiritual factors. When an embargo is placed on marriages in a particular lineage, it translates, most of the time, to lateness in marriage. Ladies especially have suffered untold agony in this area. The solution is strictly spiritual.

HAVE YOU OBSERVED THAT DIVORCE RATE IS HIGH IN YOUR FAMILY?

If you have observed that, the rate of divorce has risen astronomically you need to look into the root causes. If you have discovered that most family members have got married, divorced and married again time without number, it could be a spiritual problem. By the time it becomes an established pattern, it is clear that it is a problem that the whole family is going through.

ARE THERE IMAGES, SYMBOLS OR DEMONIC MARKS IN YOUR FAMILY?

One thing you must look out for is the presence of images, symbols and demonic marks. Most families in local communities have in their homestead all kinds of fetish images, symbols of idol worship and marks of dedication to idols. The presence of these items play some roles in the lives of family members. Since these images, marks and items belong to demons, sooner or later, they will come up with demands. Family members will be left with no options than to pay the dues. Most of the time, the dues are very costly. If the common problems you are suffering in your lineage are occasioned by the payment of dues, you need serious prayers and deliverance.

HAVE YOU EVER TAKEN NOTE OF THE MARKS IN YOUR BODY: YOUR FACE, YOUR LEGS, YOUR CHEST, YOUR HEAD AND YOUR ANKLES?

It is a common practice in Africa that there are certain marks or tattoos in the body. Most of the time, these marks are demonic symbols. They are marks of dedication to idols. They can also come in form of identification that consequently mark people out as a member of a particular race. Racial or local marks often spot people out for the attention of the guardian demons of the family.

You might have forgotten when such marks were etched into your body, but you can simply examine your face, your stomach, your legs, your chest and your head to see if you have what can be regarded as spiritual identification marks of your family. Once these marks are there, you should get ready for collective captivity. The solution is deliverance and prayers to cancel evil covenants and erase demonic marks. Let me make it clear at this point that some marks are not visible but they can be visible to satanic agents. You must make use of the fire of the Holy Ghost to rub off these evil marks. You also need to declare like Paul the Apostle saying "For I bear in my body the marks of the Lord Jesus."

DO YOU KNOW WHAT THE SYMBOLS AND THE TRADITIONAL MARKS IN YOUR BODY STAND FOR?

Most traditional marks are rooted in idol worship. In some communities, there are elaborate marks and signs on the body. These marks have deep meanings in the spiritual realm. Our forefathers had their own native occult signs. Those who belong to secret societies often carry these traditional marks to show that they belong to a powerful society. Most of the time, the effect of such marks are transferred to their offsprings.

HAVE YOU EVER TRIED TO ERASE THE EVIL TRADITIONAL MARKS IN YOUR BODY?

Some traditional marks are difficult to erase. Some were done with powerful local ink that requires serious efforts to rub off. The truth is that rubbing them off is not the only solution. You must pray to rub them off. Additionally, you need to pray against the spiritual impacts and the consequences of the marks that your forefathers bore.

ARE YOU AWARE OF THE FACT THAT THE POWERS THREATENING YOUR LIFE, DESTINY AND PROGRESS MAY BE ON YOUR SKIN?

The devil has captured many families through physical and spiritual marks. The powers threatening your life and destiny may be as close to you as the marks on your skin. Beloved, herein lies one spiritual principle. The marks on your skin can mark you out for problems. The traditional marks on your body can earmark you for spiritual arrows. The marks on your skin can be used by the devil as a demonic chip for giving you up easily as a target of attacks from the kingdom of darkness. You must destroy such marks today.

CAN YOU REMEMBER THE PRESENCE OF LOCAL IMAGES, CARVINGS AND LOCAL METALS THAT HAVE BEEN IN YOUR FAMILIES FOR GENERATIONS?

Do you often visit your country home? When you go to the village, what do you come across? Have you discovered that idols still litter where your ancestors lived? Do you know that the houses which your parents inherited and have consequently passed to you are filled with charms, amulets and various voodoo items? You might have discovered a large protective fetish at the entrance of the house, when you ask the oldest member of your family you might be shocked as you discover that such charms have been there for over 100 years. The longer such demonic items have stayed, the more demons must have used them to capture family members.

HAVE YOU THOROUGHLY EXAMINED ALL THESE THINGS?

It is important to carry out spiritual research. You must not take anything for granted. The ancestors who decided to hang the items knew what they were doing. Some of the items were put in place with heavy incantations backed up by deep promises pledging the allegiance of succeeding generations. When members of that homestead travel to either Canada, U.S.A, Europe or Asia, they remain under the spiritual umbrella put in place by the spiritual items. You must examine them thoroughly.

HAVE YOU DISSOCIATED YOURSELF FROM EACH OF THEM?

As a matter of necessity, you need to dissociate yourself from each of them. After you have located the charms or the items, you must stand up to declare that since you have been bought and redeemed by the blood of the Lamb, you can no longer have association with the idols of your forefathers. You must attack the altars spiritually and declare loud and clear that you are no longer under any covenant or spiritual union with the powers of your fathers' or mothers' house.

HAVE YOU USED THE BLOOD OF JESUS TO DRAW A LINE OF DEMARCATION BETWEEN YOU AND THESE THINGS?

You need to discover the power of the blood of Jesus. When dealing with ancestral forces, you must use the blood of Jesus as a spiritual ink for drawing a line of demarcation. Let me tell you a secret, beloved. Any line of demarcation drawn by using the blood of Jesus, is death trap for powers of darkness. That is the only power that can separate you permanently from the idols of your ancestors.

HAVE YOU DENOUNCED THE POWER OF YOUR FATHER'S AND YOUR MOTHER'S HOUSE?

You must not lose sight of the fact that ancestral powers can monitor and teleguide generations as long as they are allowed to function. Our forefathers innocently involved terrible powers and asked them to favour, protect, enrich and teleguide their offsprings. This could have lasted for hundreds of years. To get out of this evil umbrella, you need to denounce the ancestral powers of your family. When you denounce them, they will no longer have any hold upon you.

HAVE YOU RENOUNCED THE COVENANTS AND THE OATHS MADE BY YOUR ANCESTORS?

It is common knowledge that our ancestors made powerful oaths and covenants in order to obtain power and wealth from the kingdom of darkness. These oaths and covenants must be renounced. You must remove yourself from the evil consequences of oaths and covenants made with the kingdom of darkness.

HAVE YOU FORCED THEM TO DISOWN YOU?

The powers of your father's house are not likely to release you. As the Scriptures have declared, it takes the violent to take deliverance or freedom by force. You must force the power of your father's to disown you and let you go. You must make your life and destiny too hot for them to influence. You need aggressive prayers, you need hot prayers that will make evil powers disown you. When you become a spiritual prayer machine, the engine of your life will become terribly hot and strangers shall be frightened out of their closed places, at that point they will voluntarily disown you.

DO YOU KNOW THAT A LOT OF THINGS THAT WERE BURIED BY YOUR ANCESTORS IN YOUR FAMILY HOUSES ARE NOW DESTROYING YOUR DESTINY?

Buried items and charms are spiritual entities. The fact that they are buried and invisible cannot prevent them from being active. Those things that were buried decades ago might be affecting your life now. You must pray against such buried items and prevent them from destroying your destiny. Whatever your ancestors buried must not be allowed to bury your virtue. You must raise serious prayer points against whatever your ancestors buried in your family house.

CAN YOU RECALL THE IMAGES OF YOUR FATHER OR GRAND FATHER DRESSED IN EVIL COSTUMES OF HUNTERS, LODGES OR THE APPAREL OF LOCAL CHIEFTAINS?

When you visit your family house, you might discover that there are pictures of your forefathers where they are dressed in masquerade attire and costumes of lodges or hunters. Most of the time, the dresses of your ancestors were soaked in blood or in powerful charms. Such demonic costumes often affect an entire generation. When you see an image of your grandfather in the full regalia of a powerful chieftain, you should know that he was never an ordinary man. The regalia often portray the spiritual level attained in the occult.

If you remember these images when you were a child, it shows that some spiritual currents must have been transferred into your life through such powerful principalities. If you try to look at the eyeballs of your ancestors in the pictures they left behind, you might discover that they are drunk with spiritual power to the point of intoxication. You need serious deliverance.

HAVE YOU LAID YOUR SPIRITUAL HANDS ON THESE THINGS TO DESTROY THEM?

If you watch the spiritual items, charms, amulets and fetishes remain there with their full powers, the whole family will be affected spiritually by them. When you go home, you can go into fasting and spiritual warfare and specifically lay hands on the items left by your ancestors. By laying hand

on them you can cause them to expire and destroy
them. You can also pour the anointing oil on
them. At that point they will stop discharging
negative currents into the lives of members of
your family.

HAVE YOU CANCELLED THE EVIL PROMISSORY NOTES MADE BY YOUR ANCESTORS?

Your forefather made lots of promissory notes at
evil shrines. As it were, promissory notes were laid
at the altar of the power of your ancestors. These
promissory notes must be burnt to ashes
spiritually. Every pledge made by your ancestors
must be revoked by you. You must destroy every
legal tender being kept in the archives of darkness
as evidences against your entire family line.

HAVE YOU RENOUNCED THE EVIL THINGS OF DARKNESS?

You must renounce the hidden things of
darkness. Whether the oaths of allegiance were
personally made by you or previously made by
your ancestors hundreds of years before you were
born, you must renounce everything.
Renunciation will cancel the handwriting of
darkness that has remained a demonic reference
point against your family. Renunciation must be
total and complete.

HAVE YOU SANCTIFIED YOUR FAMILY NAME AND LINEAGE?

Your actions in this regard must be proactive. You must destroy the ancient order. You must put an end to the regime of darkness. But you must go further. You must raise up the banner of the Holy Spirit and specifically sanctify the name of your family as well as the name of your entire lineage. Through prayers you must purge your family from the deposits of demonic covenants. When sanctification is complete, your family will breath fresh air. Every form of spiritual pollution or contamination will disappear. The Spirit of God will sanitise the atmosphere of your family. Sanctified and purged, your entire family will begin to experience the power and the glory of God.

HAVE YOU REVOKED THE EVIL OPERATIONAL LICENSE USED BY YOUR ANCESTORS?

Are you aware of the fact that the powers of your father's house operated legally because they had in their possession an evil operational license? This license can be revoked when you invoke the thunder and fire of God against them. The moment you revoke the license their wicked activities will be brought to an abrupt end.

HAVE YOU WASHED YOURSELF SPIRITUALLY IN THE BLOOD OF THE LAMB?

You cannot do these things without immersing yourself totally in the blood of Jesus. The power of the blood of Jesus, when applied upon your life, will make your life a no-go area. The devil will no longer be able to penetrate your life. If the powers of your father's house want to launch a counter attack they will discover that you are fully immersed in the blood of Jesus. The devil will flee at the sight of the blood of Jesus. There will be no counter attack.

HAVE YOU USED THE BLOOD OF JESUS TO RUB OFF EVIL MARKS?

Physical marks or tattoos are often indelible. But there is good news for you. There is an eraser that can fully rub off satanic marks. That eraser is the blood of Jesus. You can command the blood of Jesus to become an eraser and totally remove traces of satanic marks. The blood of Jesus works wonders. It is the only power that can render evil marks null and void.

CAN YOU NOW SAY I BEAR IN MY BODY THE MARKS OF THE LORD JESUS?

After the application of the blood of Jesus as a spiritual disinfectant, there must be instant automatic replacement. The devil loves it when there is a vacuum. Herein lies your spiritual strategy, you must apply the mark of the blood of Jesus all over your body. You must get to a point when you can boldly say that there are marks of the blood of Jesus all over your body. Once that step is taken, you are free from all forms of satanic invasion.

ARE THERE SOME PLANTS THAT YOUR FAMILY MEMBERS DO NOT EAT?

You need to ask questions meticulously, if there are plants that members of your family are told to avoid, you are under bondage. As long as the plants are not poisonous there is no reason why members of your family must be told; "Do not eat this plant, do not eat that plant." Beloved, there are hidden spiritual reasons why some plants are forbidden. It is possible that the plants were used as part of concoction for powerful rituals made for or by your ancestors. Such spiritual embargo must be personally prayed over and nullified by you.

ARE THERE FOOD ITEMS THEY FORBID DUE TO PAST FETISH COVENANTS?

The Bible makes it clear that you may eat any natural food after it is sanctified through prayer. But, most of the time some families do not eat certain food. Some food items are taboo simply because they have spiritual connotations or they formed part of an ancient covenant. If family members remain under such a bondage, there will be serious consequences. If there are no scriptural reasons for avoiding a particular food item and you keep on abstaining from it, you have joined a demonic bandwagon. You need deliverance.

ARE THERE STONES, ROCKS, TREES, RIVERS AND ANIMALS THAT YOUR FAMILY WORSHIP?

The history of most local communities is replete with instances of the worship of stones, rocks and trees. Animism was entrenched in the primordial past of almost every African or Asian. If your family is still worshiping some rivers and rocks, members are still under a demonic umbrella. This kind of background will continue to keep members under spiritual slavery.

ARE THERE SOME REGULAR PARTIES AND LOCAL FESTIVALS THAT YOUR FAMILY CELEBRATES.

Rural communities have regular local festivals. The high point of such festivals is idolatry. Ancient masquerades are brought out, powerful rituals are made as the sons and daughters of the land are summoned home to pay homage to the idols of their forefathers. Big parties are thrown and there are lots of funfair. While these festivities go on, witch doctors come out in the night to invoke the idols of the land.

There could be secret human sacrifices and rituals that cannot be done during the day. If your community is still entrenched in this kind of demonic festivities, there are serious problems. You need to pull out of that kind of modern idol worship. You need serious research so that nothing will be taken for granted.

ARE THERE CERTAIN REGULAR SACRIFICE?

The issue of offering sacrifices to idols and dead ancestors is common in most families. Each time sacrifices are offered, there is serious demonic traffic in the spiritual realm. When sacrifices become regular, strong affinity is developed between members of the family and demonic spirits. In any family where sacrifices are regularly offered, it will magnetise demons and generations will be affected.

DO YOU KNOW WHAT THE SACRIFICES ARE MEANT FOR?

Sacrifices are offered in order to open channels of communication with demonic powers. Every sacrifice is an attempt to erect an altar for the devil. All the sacrifices made in your family line have records in the spiritual realm. Sacrifices are negative spiritual statements. When you offer sacrifices, you are inviting demons. You must wrest your destiny from the grips of evil powers. The effect of sacrifices must be nullified.

ARE THERE SOME DESTRUCTIVE HABITS IN YOUR FAMILY LINE?

Most of the time, the same destructive habits that were found in the lives of your ancestors are also found in the lives of all the children. Once these bad habits run through the family line, it has become a spiritual problem. Almost everyone in the lineage will exhibit such traits and any effort made to stop these bad habits may yield nothing. These bad habits should provoke you to pray hot prayers and also go for deliverance.

ARE YOUR PARENTS FETISH?

If your parents were deeply entrenched in fetish practices, you need to go through deliverance as urgently as possible. Fetish practices generally trigger complex bondages. The charms, the sacrifices and the fetish practices which your ancestors indulged in have great consequences. Once you have discovered that your ancestors were into fetish practices at any level, you should quickly go for deliverance.

ARE THERE FETISH PRIESTS AND SHRINE ATTENDANTS IN YOUR FAMILY LINE?

Some families are so deeply involved with fetish practices that they have resident family fetish priests and shrine attendants. When such attendants lived in your premises and were fed by the larger family, automatically he would have collected terrible things from the table of the devil. Such satanic officials are evil ambassadors. An evil ambassador is a representative of the kingdom of darkness. If your ancestors went as far as hiring a witch doctor or a fetish priest, it is obvious that they were deeply involved in local magic and the worship of idols. The situation is more pronounced when your own ancestors are the fetish priest or the shrine attendants. At that point, you have a situation where your ancestors were front line satanic agents, in your hands.

With that kind of background, you need serious deliverance. Generally, offsprings of witch doctors and shrine attendants struggle with poverty, deep bondage and mysterious battles. The fact that you are now born-again cannot erase your spiritual links with demons. You can only be free when you are totally delivered.

ARE YOU REALLY SURE THAT YOU ARE A LEGITIMATE CHILD?

These are serious issues. Illegitimacy has serious consequences in the spiritual realm. Any child that is born by any woman that is not scripturally married is a bastard. In many communities, there are children with no traceable father. There are times when a woman who lives with her husband knows that the child in her womb belongs to another man due to her immoral life style.

In many families, there are bastards or illegitimate children. whether you are informed or not, as long as you are a product of an illegitimate pregnancy, you will experience strange spiritual problems. Deliverance is required if you want to recover your true destiny. If your legitimacy is in doubt, you need to go for prayer.

ARE YOU FROM A POLYGAMOUS BACKGROUND?

If you are from a polygamous background, there will be a harvest of complex problems. In most African communities, polygamy was and still remains prevalent. Some men have raised children from several women. When such a father dies, five or six women will line up with their children. Polygamy has serious problems. Those from polygamous background struggle with complex problems. Their lives are characterised by instability, failure at the edge of miracles, sudden mishaps and they always struggle with minimal achievements to show for their sweat.
The solution is complete deliverance.

DO YOU BEAR NAMES LIKE ONWUBIKO, NWANKWO, OKONKWO, NWAGBARA, NJOKU, OKORONTA, OGUNDE, BABATUNDE, FASANMI, IYABO, OGUNBO, USUA, INYANG?

People with ungodly or demonic names often experience serious attacks. If your name is attached to local idols or if it is attached to names of certain demonic characters in your ancestral line, you are likely to battle with terrible attacks and mysterious problems. Demonic names go hand in hand with demonic problems.

If your name suggests that you are a reincarnation of someone in your ancestral line, it shows that the spirit of the departed has also entered your spirit. If your names mean darkness, struggle, sadness, backward, tears, etc, you should expect your life to reflect your evil appellation. Any name that does not glorify God or any name that does not speak of what is positive will surely affect you negatively. Your name can put you in bondage.

Your name can magnetise attacks and problems. You need to go for deliverance. You must severe the effects of evil names from your destiny. Do not allow the devil to push you into the valley of darkness through your name. Terrible names require drastic change of name. Your life must be secured. If each time your name is called, there is serious jubilation in the kingdom of darkness, you have serious problems in your hands. If your name runs contrary to God's expectation upon your life, you better change that kind of name. If you are named after the idol of your father's house, how do you expect angels to call that kind of name?

HAVE YOU CHECKED OUT THE MEANING OF THESE NAMES?

Answering to a name is not enough, you need to know the true meaning of your name before holding on to such a name. You need to actually ask your parents to tell you the meaning of your name. If you are named after your local market day, powerful hunters and strange witch doctors, you need to do something about it. If your name means cobra, lion, cats or any strange animals or bird, you should realise that such a name means negative things in the spiritual realm. Tell me, why should someone be named tears instead of laughter, death instead of life. Sorrow instead of joy or darkness instead of light? What has the name of human beings got to do with trees, shrines, an Ifa oracle, water, rain or forest? If from day one your name means you shall not succeed, how will you attain success? You must reject any negative factor in your name. Delay is dangerous.

IF THERE IS ANY EVIL THING IN YOUR NAME? PRAY FERVENTLY AND DISSOCIATE YOURSELF PHYSICALLY AND SPIRITUALLY FROM THE NAME

Our forefathers gave names to their children to reflect the darkness that prevailed at that time. For example, some names are attached to sorcery or witchcraft. You must raise a prayer altar to the Lord and declare that every evil attachment to your name shall not attach your destiny to the grave yard of darkness. You must dissociate yourself physically and spiritually from every evil name.

DO YOU HAVE SHRINES IN YOUR FAMILY?

A shrine is a place where spiritual powers carry out their activities. It is a spot where idols or demons are worshipped. Simply put, a shrine is the table of the devil. Whether it is located in some premises in a community or a family, a shrine is the headquarters of demonic spirits. It is the altar of darkness. It is the specific spot where evil items are carried back and forth. The presence of a shrine in your ancestral house shows that they had deep affiliations with the enemy. A shrine shows that the presence of the devil has been brought down to the family or a community.

Every shrine has invisible attendants. These attendants are loaded with power and they freely distribute problems, spiritual attacks and, of course, evil spirits to every member of the community or the extended family. You cannot expect your ancestors to provide accommodation for the devil and the devil will not demand serious payback from every members of the family. It is possible that the shrine is no more in use but you can be sure that the evil deposits that it has received for several decades must be affecting the virtues of that family.

DO MEMBERS OF YOUR FAMILY CARRY OUT RITUALS ANNUALLY?

If you belong to a large family where rituals are carried out annually, your glory could have been sold off during those rituals. Whether it is during the new Yam Festival or any other local festival, every ritual carried out is an avenue for the exchange of the glory of the family. Even if you no longer attend events where rituals are done, the fact that you are a member of the large family has put you under serious risk. It is either your prayer temperature is hot or you are regularly praying against demonic rituals that are done in your family.

ARE THERE CURSES IN YOUR FAMILY LINE? FIND OUT THE CURSES AND DEAL WITH THEM.

One of the greatest problems affecting today's generation is the problem caused by curses placed on the family. Whether the curses were put in place close to 100 years ago or it is a recent curse, you must find out thoroughly and deal with them. When members of the family are suffering mysteriously, it shows that they are caught up with mobile curses. Those who placed curses on the family took deliberate actions. The curses are also programmed to perform definite actions. Hence, when strange things begin to happen and the remote causes are traced to certain curses, the only solution is deliverance and curse-breaking prayers. Those who suffer most are members of cursed families. You must pray against known and unknown curses militating against your family. When you pray, curses are cancelled, yokes are broken and wicked burdens are lifted.

IS THERE ANY RITUAL THAT IS PREVALENT IN YOUR FAMILY AND EVERYONE IS FORCED TO PARTICIPATE?

Satanic agents do not hide their intentions. They generally come to the open to declare what they want. They want everyone to participate openly. Those who are reluctant are sometimes forced or compelled to be involved in the rituals. If rituals have been made compulsory in your family, there must be hidden reasons behind such actions. Any family where rituals are made compulsory is an attempt to spiritually enslave or put every member under bondage. If it is always war when some family members openly declare that they are not going to be present during the rituals. There are members of that family who know the pact which they signed with the devil. If you are a member of such a family, you seriously need prayer.

DO YOU EAT IN THE DREAM?

Those who eat in the dream are fed from the dining table of darkness. Any power that forces you to eat in the dream surely wants to put you under bondage. Every food eaten in the dream causes spiritual pollution.

There are demons whose responsibilities are to initiate, pollute or make their victims sick. Eaten food provided by demonic caterers opens you up to satanic attacks. Dream meals are satanic traps. Those who eat regularly in the dream will, sooner or later, fall under satanic manipulations. When you are fed with strange meals by strange persons, your spiritual life is in danger.

Most of the problems you are going through are caused by eating in the dream. Of course, when satanic agents cannot catch you in the physical realm, they will turn to evil caterers and forcefully feed you with food laced with spiritual poison. You must ask the Holy Spirit to purge your life and deliver you from any bondage caused by eating in the dream.

ARE YOU FED WITH STRANGE RITUAL FOOD?

A lot of people are going through strange battles today because they were fed with strange food in their sleep. If you often dream of being fed with strange food repeatedly, you stand the risk of spiritual pollution, oppression, evil manipulation and outright bondage. Any food eaten in the dream is not ordinary.

But, the moment it is strange food, the risk is higher. Those who are made to forcefully eat what looks like ritual food should run as far as their legs can carry them to the deliverance ground. Ritual food is meant for idols and evil spirits. The fact that you have been fed with that food shows that you are either one of them, they are trying to initiate you or they have given you part of their food in order to attack you spiritually. If you wake up and start feeling uncomfortable after eating ritual food in the dream, you should quickly vomit such food spiritually.

HAVE YOU DREAMT OF CLIMBING A STAIR CASE AND YOU ARE UNABLE TO GET TO THE TOP?

What you see in your dream reveals the kind of problems you are having in the spiritual realm. Your dream is your spiritual monitor. Your dream gives you insights into the stark realities of the unseen world. Never take your dreams for granted. Never ignore the kinds of dreams you have repeatedly. Your dreams are pictures of what happened in the past, what is happening at the moment and what will happen in the future. Most of the time, your dream shows you what you may need to avoid and the areas in which you may need prayers. For example, if you dream about climbing a stair case but you are unable to get to the top, you need to pray for power to finish well and strong. If you are not able to get to the top of the stair case in a particular dream, you need serious prayer.

HAVE YOU DREAMT OF FIGHTING WITH STRANGE PEOPLE?

Any form of fighting in a dream shows that you need to watch out for spiritual attacks. Fighting with strange people each time you dream shows that you are contending with many forces. It also shows that they are trying to attack you for one reason or the other. When strange or wicked people come with forces to attack you, you must not take it lightly. Enemies are at work ready to do battle against you. If enemies whose faces you cannot recognise are involved in physical fight in the dream, you are under spiritual attacks.

HAVE YOU DREAMT OF FALLING FROM A CLIFF OR AN UNUSUALLY HIGH MOUNTAIN?

When you dream about falling from a great height, you must pray hard. Danger is near. God is probably warning you that there is imminent danger.

DO YOU ALWAYS DREAM ABOUT FIGHTING WITH ANIMALS?

This is dangerous. Fighting with animals and beasts portends dangers. Such animals are demons in human form. They are sent to attack your destiny. It is a sign of danger to see yourself fighting with animals in your dream. You must pray against such dreams. You must also terminate the effect of such wicked invasion. When you dream about fighting human beings, it is bad, however, if you dream about having a strange brawl with animals, it is very dangerous.

DO YOU OFTEN SEE YOURSELF BARGAINING BUT BUYING NOTHING IN THE MARKET?

One indication of fighting ancestral battles is seeing yourself bargaining to purchase items in the market but buying nothing at the end. To spend hours in the market or supermarket and not buying a single item shows that your destiny is under attack. The spirit that makes you to struggle hard and purchase nothing is in operation. When you bargain and nothing is bought, you are operating under the negative anointing of failure. Bargaining and buying nothing shows that anti-destiny powers have sold you a ticket of failure. You must pray against the power that makes you to purchase nothing after spending hours in the market square of life.

DO YOU OFTEN SEE YOURSELF IN THE DREAM PUTTING ON RAGS AND WORKING BAREFOOT?

You must not allow any power to strip you of your glory. Any power that wants to make you naked must be arrested, paralysed and imprisoned. Again, you must pray against any power that wants to dress you in rags. You must pray against any power that has vowed that you shall not put on your shoes. Putting on rags is the symbol of poverty. Walking bare foot is a symbol of shame, ridicule and being robbed of one's glory. Rags show that your glory has been violated. Walking bare foot is also a symbol of suffering. Such dreams show that you are under the satanic agenda of physical and spiritual emptiness. You must resist such a dream violently.

HAVE YOU DREAMT AND SEEN YOURSELF NAKED BUT EVERY EFFORT MADE TO COVER YOURSELF FAILED?

Being naked in the dream shows that the arrow of shame has been shot against you. Every time you see yourself naked in the dream, you need serious prayer. It shows that the enemy wants to take away your glory. It is a symbol of embarrassment. It also shows that the devil is bent on removing your glory.

When you see yourself naked in the dream, it shows that the devil wants to rob you violently and leave you bare and penniless. It shows also that the enemy is interested in seeing you ravaged, hopeless and totally deprived of your benefits. If you make definite efforts in the dream to cover your nakedness but the efforts did not work, you need to declare fasting and prayer or quickly run to the deliverance ground.

DO YOU SOMETIMES SEE STRANGE MARKS AND INCISIONS ON YOUR BODY?

Strange marks and incisions show that you received strange visitors in your dream. When demons invade your dream life, leaving behind some strange marks, they want you to know that they came around to demonstrate some of their powers. You need to apply the anointing oil upon such marks. You need to spiritually invoke the fire of the Holy Ghost to rub off the signature of darkness placed anywhere on your body. You need serious prayer.

DO YOU OFTEN WAKE UP WITH PHYSICAL MARKS ON YOUR BODY WHEN YOU KNOW THAT THE MARKS WERE NEVER THERE?

If you always wake up with strange marks on your body when you know that the marks were never there, you have been under spiritual attack. It is strange if you wake up to find marks from nowhere, in some parts of your body. It simply shows that you have had demonic visitors.

Demons probably paid you a visit and decided to leave proofs of their visit behind. You should never ignore these strange physical marks. You need to pray back to sender prayers and decree that the power that puts the marks in place must do repeated summersaults and die. You need to spiritually rub the blood of Jesus all over your body and physically anoint yourself with the anointing oil.

DO YOU HAVE SEX IN THE DREAM?

Sex in the dream is a symbol of serious sexual assault. Sex dreams will always lead to sexual bondage. A lot of people are victims of spirit wife and spirit husband attacks. Those who have these kinds of dreams experience severe hindrances and marital pollution. You must pray against every form of sexual dream today.

HAVE YOU EVER DREAMT OF HAVING SEX WITH STRANGE PEOPLE?

Some people have sex with people whose faces they cannot identify in the dream. At other times, there are people who have had sex with people who are complete strangers.

Such dreams could bother on voluntary sexual intercourse, while others are victims of violent rape in the dream. Immediately you wake up, you must pray and charge yourself with Holy Ghost fire. Then you must pray sanitising prayers. Reject, bind and paralyse the strangers and draw the blood line with fervent prayers. You must also terminate the assignment of the strange sexual partners.

DO YOU OFTEN FIND YOURSELF WRITING EXAMINATIONS IN THE DREAM BUT YOU COULD NOT FINISH WRITING THE PAPERS?

This is a symbol of serious attacks. If you wake up from the dream when you are still unable to finish writing your examination, you need to pray against the spirit of abandoned projects and failure. You must overcome any satanic agent who has vowed that good things will not come to you and you will not complete any on-going project.

DO YOU SEE STRANGE BEINGS IN THE DREAM?

When strange beings appear to you in the dream, it shows that the enemy has sent them to frighten or attack you. These strange creatures must be fought to a stand-still. You must paralyse and terminate the mission of demons on assignment. You must pray and cut short the joy of the enemy. You must inflict fatal injury on them. You must command them that they should never appear to you again. Every harassing demon must be ordered to fall down and die.

HAVE YOU DREAMT ABOUT EATING FROM THE SAME PLATE WITH PEOPLE WHO ARE VERY DIRTY?

When you eat in the same plate with extremely dirty people, you have a lot of work to do. When unclean creatures dip their hands in the same plate with you, it shows that the devil wants to pollute your staff of bread.

You must invoke the fire of God upon every bird of darkness sent against you. Polluted hands and demonic spoons must be ordered to stay clear.

HAVE YOU EVER SLEPT AND WOKEN UP THE NEXT DAY ONLY TO DISCOVER THAT PART OF YOUR HAIR HAS BEEN REMOVED?

This is strange. Your hair is a symbol of your glory. Whoever cuts off your hair must be ordered to begin to cut his or her own hair. You must order every thief that has tampered with your hair to return what has been stolen. You must declare loud and clear that your hair shall not receive attacks.

You must command the fire of the Holy Ghost to incubate your hair. You must also decree that the removed hair shall not be usable.

HAVE YOU EVER DREAMT ABOUT CUDDLING AND PLAYING WITH DANGEROUS SNAKES AND ANIMALS?

There is no fellowship between animals and human beings. If you keep seeing yourself cuddling and playing with animals and snakes in the dream, you need the power of the Most High God to be set free.

HAVE YOU EVER SEEN YOURSELF BEGGING FOR ALMS IN THE DREAM?

Begging alms in the dream is a sign of poverty. It is a means used by the devil to inject poverty and lack to the lives of people. Begging for alms and receiving coins in the dream shows that a platform is being erected for poverty. You need to pray against and cancel the effect of such dream.

DO YOU OFTEN EXPERIENCE FRUSTRATION OR OPPRESSION WHENEVER YOU SLEEP?

Oppression is the handiwork of dark powers. When oppression gets to the level of affecting your sleep by giving you terrible nightmare, you are under serious attacks. When you experience disturbing oppression whenever you sleep, you need to pray against it.

HAVE YOU EVER BEEN FLOGGED BY UNKNOWN PERSONS IN THE DREAM?

When you are flogged by unknown persons in the dream, you are going through terrible attacks. When some people are flogged in the dream, they often wake up with visible marks. Such a dream should not be ignored. You need serious prayers.

DO YOU OFTEN SWIM IN THE DREAM WHEN YOU KNOW THAT IN REALITY YOU DO NOT KNOW HOW TO SWIM AT ALL?

Swimming in the dream when you have never done so physically shows that marine spirits are planning to do something negative in your life. Swimming is not a healthy activity to be done in the realm of the dream. It is dangerous when you see yourself as an excellent swimmer but you know that in reality, you do not know how to make a single stroke. You need prayer.

HAVE YOU EVER DREAMT OF SEEING YOUR DEAD BODY IN THE MORTUARY?

When you dream of seeing your corpse in the mortuary, there is cause for alarm. Seeing another person in the mortuary is bad enough. Seeing yourself dead in the mortuary shows that the spirit of death is trying to attack you. That type of negative dream must be cancelled. You must declare "I shall live and not die, I must declare the works of God." The spirit of death shall not capture your life.

DO YOU ALWAYS DREAM OF SEEING YOURSELF IN YOUR OLD PRIMARY SCHOOL?

This is a symbol of backwardness. It shows that certain powers are trying to pull back the hands of the clock. You must pray against the spirit of demotion. You must resist any power that wants to take you back to square one.

DO YOU OFTEN SEE DEAD PEOPLE, PARTNERS AND RELATIVES IN YOUR DREAM?

If your dreams centre on seeing those who died several years ago, it is an evil signal. If you regularly see those who were close to you, you are under subtle attacks by the spirit of the grave. You must decree that the dead shall no longer dominate your dreams. Declare loud and clear that there is no fellowship between the living and the dead. Cancel everything that is magnetising dead people to your dream.

HAVE YOU EVER SEEN YOURSELF IN THE DREAM TRYING TO APPROACH A DOOR ONLY FOR THE DOOR TO BE CLOSED BEFORE YOU GOT THERE?

This represents the spirit of hindrance. You need to pray against closed doors. You must pray that every hindrance projected into your life through the dream must backfire by fire. You need to ask God to open every closed door. You must pray against the powers that are trying to shut the doors of breakthroughs thereby preventing you from entering into your glorious destiny.

DO YOU SEE OLD MEN AND WOMEN WHO ARE FAR OLDER THAN YOU BOWING DOWN AND CALLING YOU KING OR QUEEN IN THE DREAM?

This portends danger. Those who have such dreams are often blind spiritually. Most of the time, they are ignorant but loaded spiritually. You must set fire on every demonic crown or staff of office. You must ask every mark of satanic royalty in your life to catch fire and disappear.

DO YOU OFTEN DREAM OF DOGS LICKING YOUR BODY IN THE DREAM?

When you see dogs in your dream, some demonic spirits are trying to attack you. When you see dogs in your dreams and the dogs are making desperate efforts to lick your body, there is something attractive that they are desperately looking for. You must cover yourself with the blood of Jesus. You need to command the fire of God to burn the dogs. Do not joke with your liberty. You must enforce your freedom.

DO YOU OFTEN DREAM OF PEOPLE SHOOTING GUN AT YOU?

Those who have this kind of dream are under serious attacks. You must pray that the weapon of darkness must not proper. You must pull down satanic strongholds.

HAVE YOU EVER DREAMT OF GIANT DOGS BARKING AT YOU?

If you ever have this kind of dream, you need serious prayer. Such a dream is a warning. You need to fast and pray. You need to do fire for fire and resist the enemy.

DO YOU WAKE UP FROM SLEEP AFTER HEARING FOOTSTEPS AT THE DOOR AND YOU CHECKED CAREFULLY ONLY TO DISCOVER THAT THERE WAS NOBODY AROUND?

What you experience in your dream is a reflection of what the enemy has planned to do. You must pray against any form of evil presence.

HAVE YOU EVER DREAMT OF HOLDING A BIBLE AND THE BIBLE DROPPED FROM YOUR HANDS?

This is an assault against your spiritual authority. It must be resisted with every energy within you. Do not allow any power to take away the word of God from your life.

DO YOU DREAM OF EATING YOUR VOMITS?

This kind of dream must be fervently refused and cancelled. You must pray against corruption. The Lord will never allow you to be disgraced. The devil shall not prosper over your life. The plan of the enemy shall be aborted.

HAVE YOU EVER DREAMT ABOUT FLYING LIKE BIRDS?

You need to reject witchcraft. You shall not be forced to become an agent of darkness. You must charge your life with Holy Ghost fire.

HAS ANYONE EVER GIVEN YOU EVIL PORTIONS, CONCOCTIONS OR FETISH WATER TO DRINK IN YOUR DREAM?

This must be resisted. You must neutralise the effect of any evil portion. You must cancel the effect of every poison.

HAVE YOU EVER SEEN YOURSELF FETCHING WATER WITH A BASKET IN YOUR DREAM?

You must reject every attempt to make your labour in vain. Ask the power of God to make you profit in every good thing.

HAVE YOU EVER SEEN YOURSELF IN A COURTROOM BEING ACCUSED AND SENTENCED TO IMPRISONMENT?

Pray against disgrace in the human court. Ask God to give you victory.

HAVE YOU EVER BEEN FORCED TO DRINK FROM A BOTTLE OR CALABASH FILLED WITH BLOOD?

Pray against satanic initiation. You need to be baptised in the Holy Ghost.

HAVE YOU EVER SEEN YOURSELF IN THE DREAM COUNTING INCOMPLETE MONEY?

Pray against any attempt to steal your portion or make you to experience partial prosperity.

DO YOU SEE STRANGE SHORT CREATURES SMILING AT YOU IN THE DREAM?

You must reject these creatures. You need to cover yourself in the blood of Jesus.

DO YOU DREAM OF RATS AND ANTS ROLLING ALL OVER YOUR BODY AND PLAYING WITH YOU?

Pray against every satanic pollution. Reject any fellowship with the kingdom of darkness.

DO YOU DREAM ABOUT WALKING AIMLESSLY IN UNKNOWN PLACES?

You must reject and cancel the curse of aimless wandering.

ARE YOU ALWAYS CHASED BY MASQUERADES IN YOUR DREAM?

Those who are chased by masquerade in the dream, most of the time, come from families where masquerades were worshipped. You need to break every covenant with masquerades in your family line. You must be spiritually charged with the fire of the Holy Spirit. Finally, you need to be thorough when dealing with these foundational problems. Do not accept anything that is less than total victory. The Lord shall fight for you.

This kind of dreams indicate that there are problems in your family tree. Although, you may not be the one that caused the problems. Your ancestors who caused the problems might have died about 100 years ago. Failure to address the problems may turn your life upside down.

HOW TO TACKLE FAMILY POLLUTION

When you fail to address the problems of pollution in the family tree, you will face the following consequences:

1. There will be fertilising problems.
2. The problems will continue to strengthen the enemy.
3. There will be evil reinforcement.
4. Stagnancy will be established.
5. Prosperity will be destroyed.
6. There will be closed heaven and iron ground.
7. There will be premature death.

Briefly let me itemise the way out:

1. Total repentance.
2. Surrender your life to Jesus.
3. Understand spiritual warfare.
4. Pray bullet prayers.

PRAYER SECTION

1. Bewitchment at the root of my life, die by fire in the name of Jesus

2. Evil effects of my parent's religion and lifestyle in my life, dry up and die in the name of Jesus

3. Resident permits of ancestral demons, be revoked by the blood of Jesus

4. Every curse of idolatry and evil effects be nullified by the blood of Jesus

5. I confront and conquer the masquerade terrorizing my family line in the name of Jesus

6. Every enemy I inherited from my father's and mother's side, destroy yourselves in the name of Jesus

7. Yoke of repeated problems, break by fire in the name of Jesus

8. Dream captivity in my life, die in the name of Jesus

9. Any evil name tying me down, loose your hold and die in Jesus' name

10. I recover every good thing I have lost as a result of my ancestry in the name of Jesus

Deliverance of the Family Tree

The family tree has played great roles in the lives of many people. Families have come under the dictates of lots of spiritual factors. In the family, generations have been tele-guided by ancestral powers. By the time research is undertaken, and the family tree of every large family is examined, we will come up with one discovery. Every family has a tree. The lives of the individual members of the family tree are ruled, controlled and tele-guided by the dominating spiritual factors in that family.

In physical terms, a tree has a root, it has a stem and branches that are adorned by the leaves and sometimes there are flowers, sometimes there are no flowers. Just as a tree is an entity, in the spiritual realm every family can be referred to as an entity or a tree. The family tree could have as many branches as possible. It is generally made up of the entire ancestral line. There is always a great ancestor who has given birth to children upon children.

THE ESSENCE OF THE FAMILY TREE

When you examine your personal family tree you will discover your great ancestor, lines of grandparents and levels of children in the family tree. However, one thing is common, the family tree has one root that has spread its tentacles deeply into the ground. Hence, certain elements run through the various stems. The root supplies nutrients for the entire tree. The moment you are part of the family tree, certain things have been supplied into your life. From your ancestral roots. Hence, members of the family often share weaknesses and strength and they also come up with similar tendencies. With this background, we are poised to understand the power and essence of the family tree.

Beloved, you are a product of a family tree. Your actions, values, attitude, moral weakness, temper and peculiarities cannot be separated from the common traits of others within the family tree. What the root supplies translates, most of the time, to your personal attitude. If the root is faulty your life is faulty. If the root is sick, the stem and leaves will be gangrened. When poison flows from the root, the branches and leaves are also poisoned. When the root is sick, the stem and branches will be sickly. Dead roots will lead to a withered tree. If you ignore the realities of the family tree you have ignored the greatest factors in life.

THE MASTER KEY

The truth concerning the family tree is the key that opens all doors. The moment you have gained spiritual insights into your family tree, life will no longer remain a riddle. You will become an overcomer. You will experience supernatural dominion. You will also become an exception to the rule. You will be able to say bye bye to foundational bondage. You will experience divine control. You will no longer bear the evil burdens of your ancestors. May God grant you deep revelations that will translate to glorious transformations in your life and destiny.

The understanding of the mystery of the family tree will give you solutions to stubborn problems, offer help to the afflicted and proffer solutions to problems emanating from long standing bondage.

> 2 Kings 15:9:
> *"And he did that which was evil in the sight of the LORD, as his fathers had done: he departed not from the sins of Jeroboam the son of Nebat, who made Israel to sin."*

This is a deep Scripture. Here, we are told of a man who did what his fathers had done. The word "fathers" appears in the plural form. It shows that the record of his evil deeds had been played out previously in the times of his fathers. The record could have been traced to as many as five or six fathers. Hence, the acts of his ancestors had been chronicled in that single verse. Here, we see a pattern in someone's family line. Beloved, most of the problems you are going through today can be found in an established family pattern that dates back to a time when you were not even born. This man did much evil in the sight of the Lord. But, the Bible makes it very clear that he was following the pattern of his fathers, unfortunately it was an evil pattern. In several families there are evil patterns. Here is my prayer for you "Any pattern of evil, demotion, tragedy and errors, you shall not follow them, in the name of Jesus."

FAMILY PATTERNS

You should take note of the patterns of your ancestors. When you see them repeated in your life it is a reminder that you must deal with your family tree. Beloved, you need to go back to your family and ask questions. Your research must cover four generations. It is possible that you have found it difficult to move to the next level because such heights are unattainable for every member of your family tree. I pray for you that any pattern of bondage and setbacks shall not be repeated in your life in the name of Jesus.

Exodus 20:5-6:
"Thou shalt not bow down thyself to them, nor serve them: for I the LORD thy God am a jealous God, visiting the iniquity of the fathers upon the children unto the third and fourth generation of them that hate me; And shewing mercy unto thousands of them that love me, and keep my commandments."

Here, God makes it clear that He visits the iniquities of the fathers upon the children. This shows that generational sins can be required in the hands of the children who did not even know when the ancestors lived. There is what is termed evil inheritance. Evil inheritance occurs when your ancestors transfer certain evil features into your life.

> 1 Kings 11:12:
> *"Notwithstanding in thy days I will not do it for David thy father's sake: but I will rend it out of the hand of thy son."*

GENERATIONAL LIABILITIES

Here, we come across the mystery of delayed judgement. There could be delayed judgement in your family line. Punishment for what your ancestors did some 200 years ago can be passed on to you. Beloved, it is possible for unborn children to be punished for the deeds of their fathers. An unborn child can inherit judgement or trouble as a result of sins committed by the ancestors. I pray; any generational liability that may cause trouble in your generation should be scattered unto desolation, in the name of Jesus.

Luke 11:50:
"That the blood of all the prophets, which was shed from the foundation of the world, may be required of this generation;"

A lot of people have wondered and lamented; why are things upside down in my life? Why do I often get into trouble? How come others are going through life without problems but things get sour when it comes to my turn? Why am I always under attack? The answer could be found in the deliverance of the family tree. Past generations can commit some sins and the present generations may receive the punishment. Today's generation can also commit sins for which tomorrow's generation will suffer.

An individual, somewhere along the family line, can commit an iniquity about 100 years ago and every family member could be suffering today. You might say this is serious. Yes it is. The problem in the garden of Eden was not with the apple or the tree, it was with the couple on ground. I pray that any generational liability that keeps you back each time you try to move forward shall be buried right now, in the name of Jesus.

THE SYMBOL

What does the family tree symbolise? The phrase family tree refers to family history. Right from the time of Adam, the devil has been throwing stones at families. The stones hit individual families in different locations. Practically, all human beings have suffered the consequences of bad family trees or family history. If you have examined your family line critically, you will discover that you have serious issues to confront. You may ignore such issues or pretend as if there are no problems, to neglect serious issues concerning your family is to mortgage your destiny. You can take the bull by the horn and decide to change the ugly trend in your family history.

It is a lamentable tragedy that most people's destinies have been ruined by their family trees. Beloved, you need to take hold of the insecticide of the Holy Spirit and begin to spray every deadly virus eating up your family tree. The satanic strategy is straight forward. He generally leads parents into errors in order to get at the children and punish them. This is a strange phenomenon I came across a terrible situation several years ago. A man came to see me with his wife and his teenage daughter. As soon as the family members entered my office they sat down and refused to say a word. There was pin-drop-silence. The man and his wife kept on looking at each others' faces. None of them was ready to say anything. After a period of silence that lasted for almost eternity, their teenage daughter opened her mouth and spoke: "I am pregnant."

Initially, I was surprised. I looked straight at her and I asked; "Young girl are you sure. Are you pregnant? She kept looking at the floor. I looked at her for the second time and said. "Okay who impregnated you?" Rather than answering my questions she kept on staring at her parents expecting them to give me an insight into that aspect of the story. When it appears that her parents would not say anything; the young lady looked at me trembling.

What came from her lips shocked me to my marrows: "It is daddy," she mumbled. At that point, I did not know what to do with the father.

It was a situation that would shock any man of God, any day. But the father had something to say, "I cannot explain how it happened. All I know is that my father did exactly the same thing "At that point, I knew that I had a generational problem to handle for that family. Something had gone wrong with that man's family tree. From his roots terrible poison was introduced to his life.

STRANGE PATTERNS

There are many who are struggling with unprintable generational problems. I remember the story of a woman who had full scale madness in her family tree. Mysteriously her four children were mad. However, they were not scavenging on the street. The first son happened to be a Ph.D. holder in mathematics. But the manifestation of his insanity was always taking place within empty classrooms. He would go into empty classrooms and halls and teach empty chairs for hours on end. The second one declared that he was a Bishop, he would go about preaching in empty church buildings. The third child established a weird supermarket where he would wake up and enter a shop where there are no goods and begin to act as if he was selling goods to non-existent consumers. The woman's last child happened to be a woman; whenever insanity spells came on her, she would enter any available bush and begin to plait hair for leaves and grasses. By the time they were brought to the deliverance ground it became clear that madness had been in their family line for decades.

Over 20 years ago, I prayed for an individual whose case was pathetic. Within one month eleven people had died in his family. I pray for you right now; any inherited captivity challenging your destiny shall be consumed by Holy Ghost fire and you shall be set free today, in the name of Jesus! The family can be likened to a republic within a republic or a world within a world. It can also be likened to a church within a church. The family is the building block of civilisation. Consequently, if things go on well in the family, things will go on well everywhere. The moment the devil captures your family, he has captured everything. You must know your family history. If you do not know your family history, you do not know anything. You are like a leaf that has dropped from a tree but you do not know where you dropped from.

KNOW YOUR HISTORY

Once the family tree is polluted or defiled the members are in trouble. Once the tree is stunted, the family tree will not be able to grow. Once there are diseases in the tree every part of the tree will suffer. Since there is no human being who has fallen from the sky, you are a product of your family tree. Injury to one member of the family is injury to all. The family tree can be likened to a chain. When one link suffers, the entire chain becomes weak.

This explains most of the stubborn problems you are facing right now. The enemy does not operate without legal rights. An innocent man could pray "Father I need a wife" Then, he dreams and the strongman of the family shows up to declare "Gentle man, I know you have prayed but there is an established fact in this ancestral line, every male has been programmed to marry a witch, so you shall marry a witch. If you are not ready to do that I hereby declare that there is no marriage." That can become the beginning of the brother's battle.

In some families, there must be members who will commit suicide.

In some families, there are individuals who must be murdered in tragic circumstances. In some families, some ladies must commit multiple abortions. In some families there is a trend of repeated miscarriages. In some families, there are instances of insanity. In some families, old members often die in strange circumstances. In some families, there are members who walk away and are never found. In some families, women marry husbands that are jobless. In some families, women do well while their husbands are poor. In certain families, there is a chain of untimely death. In some families, there are wicked members who are into occult.

DEFEATED MEN AND WOMEN

Some families have strong men and women who are sold out to the devil. What you have read so far has no respect for pastors, bishops or ministers of the gospel. The family tree is a family tree anywhere. The power of the family tree fought Abraham and defeated him. This same power defeated David. These powers floored Moses. In some families, pride, anger, arrogance and unfaithfulness are rife. In some families, members do not live long at all. Some families boast of chronic polygamy. In some families, husbands make house maids pregnant. Hereditary diseases litter some families. Some families are victims of mental delay, members of some families suffer as a result of the evil anointing of grace to grass. In some families, wives are always maltreated. In some families women lose their husband due to untimely death.

Depression, persistent fear and tragedy run through the members of some families. In some families, there is a chain of witchcraft. In some families, the prevalent problem is poverty. Every family has a purpose. Every family has a destiny. Every family has a divine agenda. As soon as the devil discovers that God's agenda for a particular family will cause trouble in his kingdom, he will do anything to prevent the family from being formed or established. If the family escapes and is consequently established, the devil will come with the agenda of satanic infiltration. Hence, is my prayer for you, every eraser that the devil has established to erase your glorious destiny, I set the eraser on fire, now, in the name of Jesus.

THE EFFECT

When the devil has planted an evil tree in the family, the following will begin to happen:
1. Disintegration.
2. Poverty.
3. Demotion.
4. Backwardness.
5. Attacks.
6. Upside down lives.
7. General confusion.

God has given us solutions to the problem of satanic attacks on the family tree. Here are the steps:
1. Surrender your life to Jesus.
2. You must repent from every known sin.
3. You must repent on behalf of your family.
4. You must wage war against termites in your family tree and pray prayers of deliverance.

Finally, make an inventory of your generational problems applicable in your situation and deal with them.

PRAYER SECTION

1. O God arise, do everything in your power to give me a new beginning in the name of Jesus

2. No matter my background, no matter my parentage, I arise and shine in the name of Jesus

3. Family curses upon my life, break by fire in the name of Jesus

4. Any battle in my life as a result of the family I come from, fall down and die in Jesus' name

5. Fire of total deliverance, burn to the root of my life, in the name of Jesus

6. By fire by fire, I escape from every evil cage over my family in the name of Jesus

7. Anything attacking the resources of my family, die in the name of Jesus

8. Darkness hanging on my family tree, depart forever in the name of Jesus

9. Mercy of God, reposition my life and family for greatness in the name of Jesus

10. By the blood of Jesus, I call forth a glorious future for my life and family in the name of Jesus

11. In the name of Jesus, I enter into my divine season

12. With the keys of David, I uncage every department of my life in the name of Jesus

13. Name yokes affecting me and my family negatively, be destroyed in the name of Jesus

14. Every mark of evil recognition in my life, be wiped off in the name of Jesus

15. Ancestral register of constant attacks, and sudden death bearing my name, catch fire and burn to ashes in the name of Jesus

16. In the name of Jesus my today is good and my future is great.

OTHER PUBLICATIONS BY DR. D. K. OLUKOYA

OTHER PUBLICATIONS BY DR. D. K. OLUKOYA

www.ingramcontent.com/pod-product-compliance
Lightning Source LLC
Chambersburg PA
CBHW060314050426
42448CB00009B/1822